by Lawrence Howard

Editorial Offices: Glenview, Illinois • Parsippany, New Jersey • New York, New York
Sales Offices: Needham, Massachusetts • Duluth, Georgia • Glenview, Illinois
Coppell, Texas • Ontario, California • Mesa, Arizona

Every effort has been made to secure permission and provide appropriate credit for photographic material. The publisher deeply regrets any omission and pledges to correct errors called to its attention in subsequent editions.

Unless otherwise acknowledged, all photographs are the property of Scott Foresman, a division of Pearson Education.

Photo locators denoted as follows: Top (T), Center (C), Bottom (B), Left (L), Right (R), Background (Bkgd)

Opener: (TL) Hulton-Deutsch Collection/Corbis, (BR) Sean Garnsworthy/Getty Images, (B) Baseball Hall of Fame Library, Cooperstown, NY; 3 Getty Images; 4 Baseball Hall of Fame Library, Cooperstown, NY; 5 Baseball Hall of Fame Library, Cooperstown, NY; 6 Getty Images; 8 Bettmann/Corbis; 10 ©Comstock Inc.; 11 Getty Images; 13 Getty Images; 14 Hulton-Deutsch Collection/Corbis; 15 Getty Images; 16 Sean Garnsworthy/ Getty Images; 17 Baseball Hall of Fame Library, Cooperstown, NY; 18 ©Comstock Inc.; 19 Harry How/Getty Images; 21 Adam Pretty/Getty Images; 22 Sporting News/ Contributor/Getty Images;

ISBN: 0-328-13513-5

7 8 9 10 V0G1 14 13 12 11 10 09 08

Facing Challenges

It is always challenging to be a great athlete. A great athlete must be smart, skillful, and fit. He or she must possess superior self-control and confidence. Even while they're struggling through adversity, the greatest athletes must find a way of masking their weaknesses from their opponents.

In the past, being an African American athlete was especially challenging, as laws did not always give African Americans the same rights as other Americans. Before the 1960s, African Americans in many places were not allowed to eat in the same restaurants as white people, or go to the same public schools. Even the most celebrated and beloved African American athletes were forced to submit to blatantly unfair regulations and restrictions.

Conditions in our society have greatly improved since that time. Yet African American athletes still occasionally face **discrimination,** or unfair treatment.

This is the story of some great African American athletes. Keep reading to find out about the challenges they faced, how they overcame them, and their amazing accomplishments.

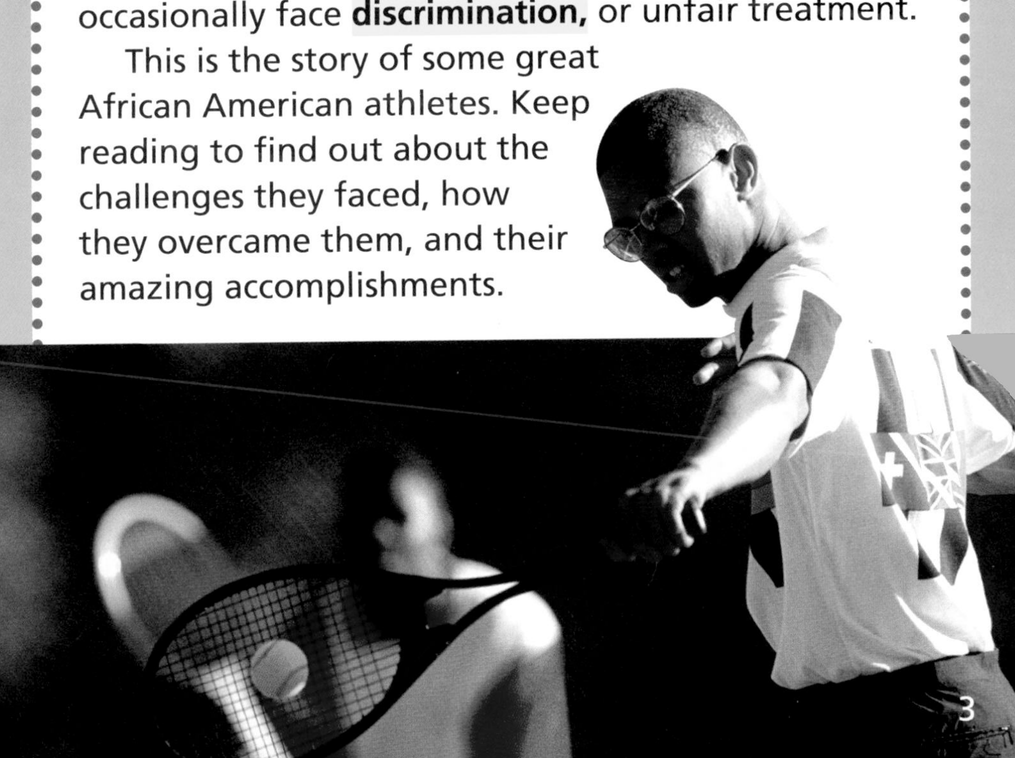

Paige, Gibson, and "Cool Papa"

Satchel Paige was a remarkable African American baseball player, and many baseball experts and fans have hailed him as the best pitcher ever. Paige was legendary both for his overpowering fastball and for his amazing stamina. He once pitched a mind-boggling twenty-nine games in one month! Paige was also famed for possessing a unique assortment of pitches. He designated many of his pitches with whimsical names, such as bee ball, jump ball, trouble ball, and Long Tom. For one of his pitches, the hesitation pitch, Paige would pause in the middle of his windup before releasing the ball to the plate.

African Americans were **prohibited** from playing in the major leagues before 1947. Because of that, Satchel Paige pitched for twenty-two years in the Negro leagues, which were set up for African Americans. Finally, in 1948, the Cleveland Indians signed the forty-two-year-old Paige to pitch for their ball club. Even at that relatively advanced age, Paige was good enough to throw for a major league franchise. But his best playing days were behind him.

James Thomas Bell, nicknamed "Cool Papa," was a great center fielder who tore around the basepaths with blazing speed. The Baseball Hall of Fame asserts that he was perhaps the fastest base runner ever. But Bell, being an African American, was denied the chance to demonstrate his brilliant talents in the major leagues.

Josh Gibson was one of the greatest hitters in baseball history. Although the Negro leagues failed to keep accurate statistics, it's estimated that he hit eight hundred home runs. Many feel that if he'd been given the chance to play major league baseball, Gibson would have eclipsed Babe Ruth as the game's most feared slugger!

"COOL PAPA"

African Americans in Basketball

African Americans were barred from participating in National Basketball Association (NBA) games until 1950. Marques Haynes and Willis Oliver were two great basketball players who happened to be African American. Even during the height of their careers, they were banned from NBA play. Fortunately, Haynes and Oliver were able to display their skills to the world by suiting up for the Harlem Globetrotters, a team of brilliant African American basketball players that toured the country competing against (and invariably beating) whichever teams would play them.

In 1950, Earl Lloyd became the first African American man to play in the NBA. Before joining the NBA, Lloyd had played college basketball brilliantly at West Virginia State College.

Lloyd was well known for his courage and determination. When asked about the poor treatment he had received because of his race, Lloyd replied that the **adversity,** or difficulties, that he faced made him a better person.

HARLEM GLOBETROTTERS

Football: The First Thirteen

From 1920 to 1933, thirteen African American men were allowed to play football in the National Football League (NFL). Starting in 1934, however, African Americans were barred from the league. They would not be allowed to play again until 1946.

Ray Kemp was one of those thirteen men. Kemp, who played the position of tackle, showed great patience with prejudiced coaches and players. He did not want to jeopardize the chance for African Americans to play in the NFL in the future.

Another one of those first thirteen was Joe Lillard. A sports reporter for a Boston newspaper said that Lillard was one of the best football players he had ever seen. Lillard was great at catching, running, and kicking the football. Unfortunately, Lillard's greatness worked against him. Some white players complained about having to play against someone so skilled.

Abe Saperstein founded the Harlem Globetrotters in 1926. They have played basketball for thousands of fans worldwide ever since.

Willie O'Ree: Blind to Failure

Willie O'Ree was born in the Canadian province of New Brunswick in 1935. Like most Canadian boys, he cared a lot about hockey. O'Ree became a very good hockey player who was known for his speedy skating. He was also a black athlete competing in a sport that was (and still is) dominated by white men.

O'Ree rose quickly through the ranks of the Canadian minor league hockey system. Then, while playing for the Kitchener-Waterloo Canucks during the 1955-1956 hockey season, he was struck by a hockey puck and lost sight in his right eye.

Despite the injury, O'Ree was determined to play in the National Hockey League (NHL). He changed his style of play to make up for his loss of sight, and continued to improve his game. At the start of the 1957-1958 season, the Boston Bruins brought O'Ree into their training camp. On January 18, 1958, O'Ree took to the ice for the Bruins against the Montreal Canadiens, becoming the first African American to play in an NHL hockey game.

O'Ree played in only forty-five NHL games, but he will be forever remembered for overcoming both his partial blindness and the **taunts** and abuse he suffered at the hands of opposing teams' fans and players. Said O'Ree: "I was determined that I wasn't going to be run out of the rink."

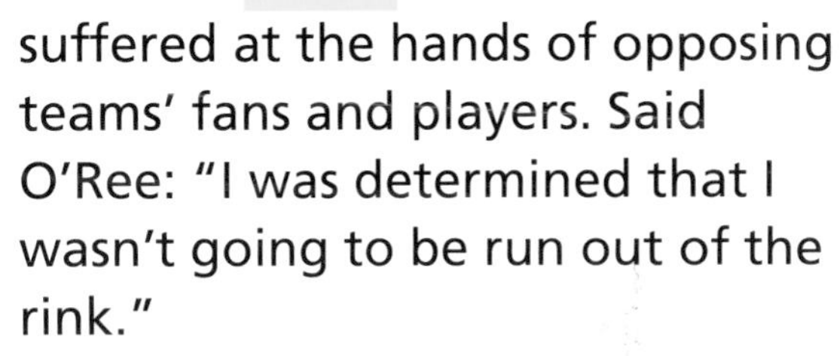

In 1998, O'Ree was appointed Director of Youth Development for NHL Diversity. And on March 25, 2003, he was given the Lester Patrick Trophy in honor of his "outstanding service to hockey in the United States."

Willie O'Ree refused to let his partial blindness, or his race, get in the way of playing professional hockey.

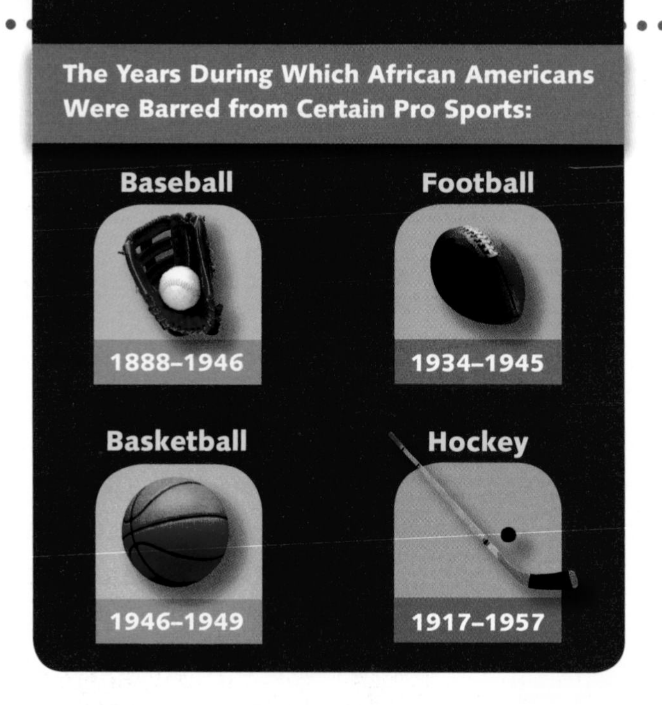

Jackie Robinson: Hero to All

Exclusion from sports was not the only challenge African American athletes faced. Many were called rude names and threatened in person, by phone, and by mail. Fans who were **prejudiced**, or disliked African Americans for irrational reasons, were not the only ones to do this. Coaches and owners of other teams also insulted African American athletes. Even reporters and their own teammates were not above berating them.

Jackie Robinson is one of the best examples of an African American athlete who faced these challenges. In the 1940s, Branch Rickey, the owner of the Brooklyn Dodgers, wanted to bring an African American onto his baseball team. He knew there were great African American baseball players who could help his team win, but he would be breaking a long-standing rule that barred African Americans from playing in the major leagues.

Because he was the first African American to play in the major leagues, Jackie Robinson made the cover of *Time* magazine.

Rickey knew that the man he selected would have to be more than just a great player. The first African American major league baseball player would need almost unlimited courage and patience to deal with the adversity he would face. Rickey watched many players before choosing Jackie Robinson for this important and risky opportunity. Robinson played his first major league game on April 15, 1947.

At first, some of the Dodgers said they would not play with Robinson, but as they got to know him, they began to respect him.

Some fans and players called Robinson bad names and spat on him. He was sent threatening letters in the mail. When Robinson was out on the field playing second base, opposing teams' baserunners deliberately hit him with their cleats when they slid into the bag; when he came up to the plate to bat, pitchers intentionally aimed their throws at his head.

Despite all these attacks, Robinson did not show hatred or anger. He did not even answer back.

Jackie Robinson's teammates, after first saying they would not play with him, grew to respect him.

It was years before every major league team allowed African American players. But because of Robinson's success, other African Americans were soon brought on by other teams. By the early 1960s, the baseball world was comfortable with having African American players.

For all that he endured, Robinson proved himself a great human being as well as a great baseball player. Millions of people came to recognize and respect him as a hero who broke down barriers in the game of baseball.

Jesse Owens: Gold Medal Winner

Jesse Owens was one of the best track and field athletes ever. In 1936, Owens went to Germany to compete in the Olympics with the U.S. team.

At the time, Germany was controlled by Adolf Hitler. Hitler thought African Americans were **inferior** to, or not as good as, the "pure" Germans of white, non-Jewish ethnic backgrounds. He did not want to see African American athletes win any medals.

Owens didn't care. He won four gold medals at the 1936 Olympics. In the process, he broke several records and embarrassed Hitler by beating the athletes from Germany.

Owens should have enjoyed an easy life after his victories at the 1936 Olympics. Sadly, racism in his own country prevented him from doing so. For years after his Olympic victories, the only way Owens could make money was by racing against horses and dogs. He commented, "People said it was insulting for an Olympic champion to run against a horse, but what was I supposed to do? I had four gold medals, but you can't eat four gold medals."

JESSE OWENS

Marshall Taylor: Ride to Glory

Marshall Taylor, an African American from Indiana, was a champion cyclist in the late 1800s and early 1900s. He won many races and set countless records.

He also had to live with the reality of racism. As a boy, he was not allowed to join the local YMCA with his friends who were white. Marshall and his friends protested, but the rules were not changed. It was Marshall's friends who gave him a bicycle to show their support.

When Marshall began racing, other racers would push or block him to keep him from winning. Despite such challenges, Taylor became a world champion at age twenty. He later became the first African American member of an **integrated**, or mixed-race, professional cycling team.

MARSHALL TAYLOR

Hank Aaron: The Home Run King

Henry "Hank" Aaron was one of the best major league baseball players of all time. He is best known for having broken Babe Ruth's record for the most home runs in a career.

By 1973, Aaron, who played for the Atlanta Braves, had hit enough home runs to practically guarantee that he would break Ruth's record. Some white fans thought it would be awful if an African American broke the record set by the beloved Ruth, who was white. Because of this prejudice, Aaron received many hundreds of pieces of hate mail each week from angry racists. However, when Aaron finally broke Ruth's record in 1974, most fans cheered him on.

In 1976 Hank became an executive for the Atlanta Braves, and later took the position of vice president. He was elected to the Baseball Hall of Fame in 1982.

Aaron has received numerous other awards and honors in his life. Included among them are a resolution by the U.S. Senate in 1999, congratulating him on his "great achievements" in baseball and his commitment to young people, and the Hank Aaron State Trail in Wisconsin, dedicated in his honor in 2000.

HANK AARON

Tiger's Tale

Tiger Woods has not faced as many obstacles as earlier African American athletes. Born in 1975, he grew up during a time when people were far more committed to treating African American athletes with the respect they deserved.

From an early age, Tiger displayed great athletic skill. By the time he was two, he was hitting golf balls. Between the ages of eight and fifteen, he won the Optimist International Junior Golf Championships an incredible six times. Few African Americans have ever played golf in its professional ranks. But Tiger received a great deal of support and financial backing from his parents, which helped his golf game immensely.

While playing as an **amateur,** or someone who does not play for money, Tiger won ten collegiate golf events, including an NCAA title. This was in addition to being named the *Golf Digest* Player of the Year in 1991 and 1992, and *Golf World* Player of the Year in 1992 and 1993.

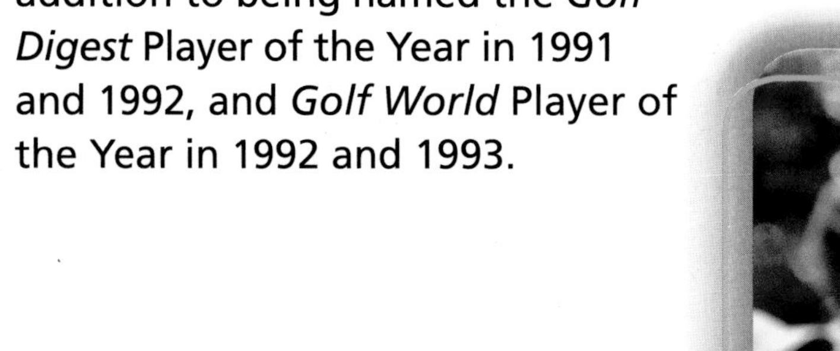

In 1996, Woods decided to move on from Stanford in order to pursue a career as a professional golfer. Following that, he became the first player since 1990 to win two tournaments in his first year as a professional. But that was just the beginning.

In 2001, Woods became the first professional golfer to hold all four major golf championships at the same time, after winning the Masters Tournament, PGA Championship, U.S. Open, and British Open. Woods has had more victories than any active golfer and has made more money playing golf than anyone in history.

Tiger has achieved some amazing records. But perhaps what is most impressive about his golf career is this: Although there have been African American golf champions in the past, Woods remains the only African American golfer who regularly competes in professional golf tournaments.

Helping to Hit the Slopes

African American athletes have been slow to take up certain winter sports like skiing and figure skating. But more opportunities are now opening up for African American athletes looking to participate in these sports. They have begun to form their own organizations to pay for equipment, lessons, and other expenses.

One of these organizations, the National Brotherhood of Skiers, strives to find, train, and support talented African American athletes who want to win international winter sports competitions such as the Olympics. The National Brotherhood of Skiers has spent over one million dollars to train African American racers to be chosen for the U.S. Ski Team.

Suki Horton could be the first African American on the U.S. Ski Team.

Suki Horton: Skiing to Success

The U.S. National Ski Team was formed seventy-five years ago. In that time, there has never been an African American competitor. Many people think Suki Horton will be the first. One of the directors of the team says that if Suki works hard and continues to improve, she has a very good chance of making the team.

Stories like Suki's are inspiring. They demonstrate that African American athletes are competing more and more in today's sports world. Thanks to the efforts of many brave athletes, the playing fields are becoming level.

SUKI HORTON

Now Try This

What If You Were Jackie Robinson?

It was no accident that Jackie Robinson was the first African American to play major league baseball. Branch Rickey had dreamed for years of introducing an African American player to the major leagues. He scouted many talented players, some more physically gifted than Jackie Robinson, before choosing Robinson.

It was Robinson's character, as much as his baseball skill, that made him ideal as the first African American major league baseball player. You have read about many of the challenges he faced in his career. He proved that Branch Rickey chose the right man for the job. If you could interview Jackie Robinson, what would you ask him?

Here's How to Do It!

Imagine that you are a reporter for a major newspaper in the late 1960s. Your editor tells you to interview Jackie Robinson about his career as a baseball player.

Write a description of how you would interview Robinson about the obstacles that he faced. Use the suggestions below to help organize your ideas.

1) Before you meet Robinson, use the Internet or other sources to research his life and career.

2) Are there any questions that you can think of, based on what you have read about him? Write them down.

3) Write down any other interesting questions that come to mind.

4) Share your questions with a classmate, then listen to the questions they thought of. You can trade ideas on how to improve your questions before the "interview."

Questions to ask Jackie Robinson

Glossary

adversity *n.* condition of misfortune or distress.

amateur *n.* someone who plays something for pleasure, instead of for money or as a profession.

discrimination *n.* act of showing an unfair difference in treatment.

inferior *adj.* below others in importance or value; low in quality.

integrated *adj.* when a public place or group has been opened to all races.

prejudiced *adj.* having an unreasonable dislike for someone or something.

prohibited *v.* forbidden by law or authority from doing something.

taunts *n.* mocking or insulting remarks; jeers.